How to be creative and change your life

Ten different ways to develop
creative ideas

About the Author

Ruchi Zindal is a former lecturer, re-searcher, visionary in light and colour therapy. She is also a creativity expert and motivational speaker. She works as a colour therapist and conducts workshops and seminars about unleashing your creative potential. She is a registered member of the reputed International College of Holistic Medicine (ICHM), England.

- She has completed her diploma in colour therapy and Iridology from the reputed School of Natural Health Sciences, London.

- Diploma in colour Therapy from S.N.H.S., London recognised by International college of holistic medicine.

- Diploma in Iridology (A grade with distinction) from S.N.H.S., London.

- She has conducted research on brain and mind healing. Currently, she is conducting workshops & seminars on how to unleash creative potential. Her work is based on pure scientific principles. She is a visionary in light therapy and colour therapy.

• Ruchi Zindal is a qualified lecturer in Economics. She has done her post graduate in Economics.

She wrote this book to help people understand the importance of creativity and how they can make their life better by exploiting it. Most people think that creativity belongs to people from a specific category like music, dance, painting, etc. but this is not correct. Each and every one of us is creative. Creativity is a hidden treasure that should be used in the right manner. When we utilize our creative abilities, we get inspired to step out of our comfort zone and take risks to fulfill our dreams. We gather the courage to follow our passion and share our creative ideas with the world. Innovations and discoveries are the results of unleashing our creative potential. Ultimately, this is the author's aim and that is why she was inspired to write this book.

Creativity is a slightly complex concept and still, there is a lot of research being done on the subject worldwide. In this book, the author has tried to make people understand these concepts in a new and easy way. She has highlighted the lives of some creative individuals and tried to show how these celebrities' accomplishments are relevant in this context. She has given the readers different methods to develop new ideas, which we can apply in our daily lives. The more we use these methods, the more creative ideas, success and happiness we can achieve.

How to be Creative and Change Your Life

Ten different ways to develop
creative ideas

Ruchi Zindal

ZORBA BOOKS

ZORBA BOOKS

Publishing Services in India by Zorba Books, 2019

Website: www.zorbabooks.com
Email: info@zorbabooks.com

Copyright © Ruchi Zindal

ISBN 978-93-88497-52-7
E-Book 978-93-88497-53-4

Zorba Books Pvt. Ltd.(opc)
Gurgaon, INDIA

Acknowledgments

I want to say a big thank you to my uncle, Mr. Shailesh Jain, who encouraged me to follow my passion and guided me every step of the way when I needed him. My husband, Tarun, and son, Akshay took personal interest in my writing. They encouraged me to do better. I want to give thanks for their valuable advice. My parents have been my lifeline. They acted like angels who watched over me constantly during the process. I am very fortunate to have them as parents and will be grateful to them forever.

Table of contents

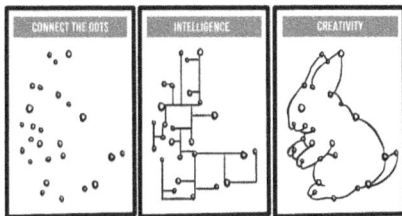

Chapter 1

Introduction

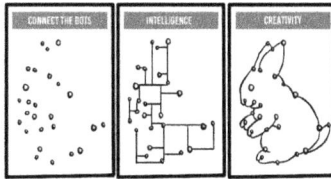

Thank you for buying this book. If you want to do something different and feel a void inside you, you are on the right track. When you read this book, you will discover your creative story. If you want to inspire others, you need to motivate yourself first. If you want to make others happy, then first and foremost, you need to be a happy person yourself.

We are all born happy and creative but we don't experience happiness because we don't utilize our creative potential. Have you thought about why we don't feel happy and content with our lives? Why we blame others for our failures or why we feel helpless and worthless? It is because we are not creative. We don't know our full potential. We don't trust our capabilities to achieve our desires. Instead, we try to do things to satisfy our family and friends. Sometimes we want recognition from family and friends so we try to earn more money, fame, etc. to make them happy.

We don't do what we would love to do. If we follow our desires, we can exploit our creative potential. However, we want to remain within our limited thinking pattern. Because we tend to suffer from fear of failure and rejection from family and friends if we do something different and out of society's norms, it blocks our creative potential. Sometimes, we don't want to take a risk to implement our new ideas due to the fear of losing money in our new business venture because we fear that people will not accept new ideas easily. If we want to turn our desires into reality, we should become fearless and have the courage to take risks. We will then be able to exploit our full potential. This will bring us peace and happiness.

We don't get happiness from genetic predisposition. We attain it

4

from our surrounding environment. Our subconscious mind works like an operating system, and our operating system has no programming at the time of birth. We download our subconscious programs according to our environment. If our environment is positive, we download positive subconscious programming which promotes healthy and positive emotions. It may be possible that our subconscious mind gets negative feedback from our environment as well. It develops our negative thinking patterns like fear, low self-esteem, self-denial, anger, sadness, self-criticism, etc. However, it does not mean that if we change our external environment, we will be positive and happy. That depends on our inner self. When our limited and negative thoughts turn into healthy emotions like love, empathy, gratitude, courage and forgiveness, it will unlock our creative potential and we will be able to think outside the box. We become courageous and fearless and we can achieve whatever we desire. So, positive thinking is a precondition to unlocking one's creative potential.

Our happiness does not depend on what others think and what we own. It depends on how we interpret life. When we do what we love to do, we become aware of ourselves, the purpose of our life and the ways to achieve happiness. We become happy and content. For example, if we are in a job but love to do something else that is creative, like painting, then we don't feel any excitement in our job or profession because we are not happy or emotionally charged. Therefore, we crave more emotional highs and happiness. And thus, we feel unhappy and unsatisfied.

Happiness can be triggered by passion, love or relationship or other types of challenges that we want to overcome. These triggers work as creative inspiration. They spark our creativity. These creative inspirations make us happy. For example, if a sportsperson does not play his favourite sport but instead works at another job due to circumstances or financial difficulties, he will be dissatisfied and unhappy. He is earning more money in the job compared to playing his favourite sport. However, only making money does not make us happy. If he plays the game he likes with passion, he can earn more money, fame and happiness as well.

Happiness depends on our self-awareness, personality, behaviour, positive emotions, environmental support, etc. Sometimes we are not aware and do not observe our emotions, thoughts and behaviour. Sometimes we don't get enough support and encouragement from our parents and peers. Due to a lack of self-awareness and a nurturing environment, we are forced to do something that we don't want to do. We find ourselves in hopeless and helpless situations and we suffer from forms of abuse and trauma. Many people sink in the mud of drug addictions and alcoholism because they can't accept their sufferings; many try to commit suicide in order to avoid their sufferings. It blocks our creative path and deprives us of happiness.

To achieve happiness, we should know who we are, what we love to do and how to achieve what we want. we need to believe in ourselves and we should be aware of our emotions, thoughts, behaviours. it brings change in our perceptions about ourselves and our surroundings. we try to change our negative thinking pattern In this process, we make our unconscious into conscious. And then we will get what we want.

Chapter 2

Creativity follows self-awareness

Creativity means generating and implementing ideas that contain elements of newness, originality and appropriateness. It is when we connect our small, new and original ideas to each other and create a whole big concept from it or combine pre-existing ideas into new combinations and create a broad original idea out of this. According to the Merriam-Webster dictionary, creativity can be defined as 'the quality of being creative' or 'the ability to create, that is, to make new things or think of new ideas'. It means that creative ideas contain two elements – originality, which was not there before, and appropriate means these ideas should be relevant, useful and have value as well.

Creativity follows up self-awareness. It means a personal understanding of who we are, a vision of where we want to go and a commitment to do to whatever is required to attain our goal. It can be a long and time-consuming process because it depends on our goal, our efforts, self-confidence, courage and our financial and other resources; it also depends on the environment. Until we are aware of our abilities and trust our intuition, our creative potential cannot be utilized. it locks our creative potentials. We will not able to connect and implement our ideas and follow our intuition. Consequently, we are unable to achieve our goal and true happiness. We live in ignorance as we don't realize our creative abilities. We don't understand who we are and what our positive strengths are.

When we are self-realized, we are connected to our inner voice or intuition and we recognize our full potential or capabilities. We don't think of ourselves as a victim of circumstances; instead we believe we are masters of our destiny. the source of self realization invisible in our surroundings. It can be family, friends, a spiritual leader or other inspirational personalities. When we are unhappy about our past, we want to resolve it, and in trying to come up with an answer to our question, we need inspirational energy or a trigger point to resolve our past and move ahead. When we get our inspirational trigger point from our environment, we are motivated and challenged to do something creative. This new understanding leads to new awareness and we find new insights to resolve our past and understand the root causes of our past problems. It leads to creative solutions.

The life story of Oprah Winfrey is a creative inspirational story. Oprah is a well-known personality and her talk shows are watched globally. She covered a variety of subjects on her shows, including topics like abuse and rape. Oprah's mother was a housekeeper who got pregnant in her teens. She left Oprah with her grandmother. The young girl spent six years with her grandmother, who was strict and supportive but abusive too. Sometimes, her grandmother would beat her. They went to church regularly. Her grandmother taught her to read and asked her to recite verses from the Bible. She recited them perfectly and so she was nicknamed 'Ms. Preacher'. Oprah says that this is where she gained her self-confidence and honed her talent to communicate with people.

When she was six years old, she went to live with her mother. They were very poor. Oprah wore potato sacks cut into dresses because they didn't have any money to buy clothes. Due to her long working hours, her mother couldn't pay any attention to her. Oprah went to the local high school but again, poverty got in the way. She was bullied and abused psychologically. During her teenage years, she was sexually abused by her cousin, an uncle and a family friend on different occasions.

At 14, Opera brought a child into the world. But her son died shortly after birth. Oprah and her mother would constantly fight with each other. So her mother sent her to her father, Vernon Winfrey. Her father gave her a new life. He brought self-realization within her. She was able to understand who she was and what she wanted out of life. He encouraged her and taught her to trust in her capabilities. She started studying and received academic awards.

She got a job at the local radio station and started working long hours. She was later hired to anchor the local television news. Her presence raised the audience rating in each show she participated in. Eventually, she was hired to co-host a talk show and then to present her own show.

The most frequent topics of discussion on Oprah Winfrey's talk shows were on molestation and sexual abuse. The show, based in Chicago, changed the image of daily talk shows. The show began to discuss more relevant topics like current news, current issues, diseases and their implications, and human rights stories. She also advocated the rights of women, the LGBT community and especially, children's causes. Big celebrities, including sports stars, actors and actresses, politicians, etc. took part in the show. The show was so popular that the Oprah Winfrey show became a household name. She also became a producer, actress and philanthropist.

Oprah spent her childhood in poverty, she faced abuse, she was molested, she did drugs but, despite all the challenges she faced, she was successful in leaving that life behind. Her half-sister, Patricia, who lived with her mother, died due to cocaine addiction and her younger brother, Jeffrey, died of AIDs, but Oprah was positive and courageous and chose to fight against all the odds. Her father nurtured her with his love and acceptance; this nurturing environment instilled in her self-confidence and courage and gave her faith and trust in herself to pursue her creative inspiration. Oprah realized her creative potential and utilized it. She forgave and forgot her past; only then was able to get ahead in her life.

In her talk shows, she discussed the causes and effects of rape and abuse and understood the difficult circumstances concerning the subject. She shot to fame and won many awards. She was the only North American black billionaire at that time.

Chapter 3

Creativity turns adversities into opportunities

Adversities come in our lives in many ways. These adversities can arrive in the form of illness, the death of a loved one, loss of life, divorce, financial difficulties, accidents and undesirable events in life. these advesities enhance our stress .we get trapped in negative thinking pattern. We think about what we don't want instead of what we want and we get distracted from our goal. this negative thinking pattern blocls our creative potential. It increases the obstacles to achieve our goal. The more we try to come out of these adversities, the more we get trapped in a vicious cycle. We suffer from anxiety and depression.

Creativity is an effective strategy against stress. It diverts our mind from stressful thoughts. Creative activities like sports, writing, painting, dancing, and music, etc. enhance self-esteem, hope and social interactions, and reduce feelings of shame, guilt, anger and rejection, especially in times of trouble. Creativity is a process of emotional and intellectual development. These developments give us the ability to deal with negative emotions related to our adversities and help us focus on achieving our goal and persevering. Creativity is like mindfulness and it encourages us to do what we want. It requires focus and attention. Creative activities like drawing, painting, playing sports, reading, writing, dancing or playing an instrument increase our focus and attention. Creativity protects us during adversities and turns adversity into opportunities.

J.K. Rowling's success is an inspiring story of how we can turn our adversities into opportunities. She is the first billionaire whose main source of income is writing. She authored the multi-awarded 'Harry Potter' book series, selling millions per installment. Her net worth is said to be more than that of the Queen of England.

Her life has had huge ups and downs. J. K. Rowling was born to Peter James Rowling and Anne Rowling. She went to Exeter University where she studied French and classic literature.

Her struggle started in her teenage years when her mother suffered from multiple sclerosis. Her relationship with her father was not cordial. In 1990, her mother died. Rowling went to Portugal and taught English as a second language to locals.

She married journalist, Jorge Arrantes but after a few years of marriage, they were divorced. She had a three-year-old daughter, Jessica Isabel. Rowling decided to live near her sister. She lived with government assistance but it was a struggle for her. She became depressed and attempted suicide more than once. The idea of Harry Potter came to her while she was on a train from Manchester to London. She began writing children's fantasy stories – the Harry Potter series.

She had started writing six years before the publication of her first book. She continued writing despite all the challenges she faced of her mother's passing, her divorce and her return to her sister's place. Rowling's writing draws from her personal experiences. She put her emotional experiences with family and friends into her magical world. After six years of writing, the first installment of the best-selling series was ready to be released. But most of the publishers turned down her manuscript.

A year later, her book was published but the publisher was not too optimistic about it and told her that she should consider getting a real job. In six months, the wheel of fortune turned over. The Scottish Arts Council awarded Rowling a grant to continue writing the Harry Potter series because they were so impressed with her work.

He fantasy stories of Harry Potter, Ron Weasley and Hermione Granger's adventures in Hogwarts received a multitude of awards from credible accrediting bodies. The books were named best-selling stories in various literary charts and by publishers all over the world. All seven of the Harry Potter books have topped the 'New York Time's bestsellers' list.

J.K. Rowling's life is a good example of how focus and patience work wonders. In life, you face many adversities but if you focus on what you want, have patience and motivation and you persevere, then wonders can happen. Our deathly adversities can turn into life-giving opportunities. This is what happened with Rowling. She kept writing despite all the difficulties she faced. Her creative writing absorbed her emotional turbulence and she maintained her focus on what she wanted. She was able to get new opportunities in writing children's fantasy books and attained the heights of creative achievement.

Chapter 4

Creativity makes self-transformation possible

Self-Transformation or personal transformation can be a life-changing experience because we change our thinking, feeling and behaviour. In this process, we change our personal beliefs and state of being. When we embrace new thoughts, actions and feelings, we create a new personal reality for our future. When we decide to do something different, which is new and original, we need to become someone else.

To become someone else, we will have to embrace new thoughts, new actions and new feelings and this is what will create a new personal reality. It sparks our creativity. We leave our known past and enter into a new, unknown and unpredictable future. Creativity helps us to move away from our old predictable past to a new and unpredictable future.

Creativity helps us to make change possible. It inspires us to change our thoughts to attain happiness and build a better future.

Our brain contains 75% water and 100 billion nerve cells (neurons). Our thinking brain (neocortex) has 10,000 to 40,000 connections per neuron. Each neuron is a biocomputer with more than 60 mega-bytes of Ram. It can process up to hundreds of thousands of functions per seconds. So by changing our thoughts, we can build a new personal reality and can enter into our new imagined future.

Our old thoughts build up during our growing years and take strong root in our mind. Due to these old thoughts, we are lost in the past and anticipate the same future. Our past is known and predictable, so something new cannot be created from the known past. New thoughts can be developed from the unknown and the unpredictable, which gives it a ring of uncertainty. It is our creative potential which has to be exploited. Until we exploit our creative potential, we cannot develop something new. The more we enter into unknown and uncertain dimensions, the more we develop our new creative thoughts.

We fire new neural activation in personal transformation. To fire new neurons, we have to understand our old thoughts patterns, behaviour and beliefs and have to consider how these affect our lives in negative ways. In this process, we make our unconscious conscious. This brings us self-awareness. We realize our true purpose in life and trust our intuition. It sparks our creativity. We are enthusiastic about the process of self-transformation and thus, we become a new person.

This change can be anything - whether a career change, a desire to leave an abusive relationship or wanting to quit a bad habit like alcohol, drugs, binge eating or an unhealthy lifestyle, etc. If we admit our past mistakes and try to break our emotional attachment to the past and make a firm decision to change it and believe that it can be possible, it will help us to build a new neural connection that was not there before. It promotes creative ideas that are new and original and leads us on the new creative path of success and happiness.

To make changes or undergo a personal transformation, we need to change negative thinking patterns like fear, self-doubt, anger and resentment into positive thinking patterns like determination, courage, gratitude, forgiveness self-acceptance, etc. Creativity helps us to make that self-transformation possible, if we focus on positive thoughts. It is not possible to make changes in our personality without changing our thoughts.

After self-transformation, we use our creative ideas to do something valuable and good for others. We want to share our ideas with the world because it makes us happy. We are inspired to educate others with our knowledge and experiences, because we think that what we have learned can change people's lives. Thus we spread this happiness to others also. We should turn our weakness into strength. We should maintain focus and persevere in the self-improvement process, not letting anything distract us from our path. We should remain in the present moment.

Anthony Robbins's story is synonymous with self-transformation that requires courage, determination, fearlessness, self-belief and perseverance. He is well-known in the field of self-improvement. Once, Robbins said, "The past does not equal to the future."

Anthony Robbins's family was very poor and his mother had multiple romantic partners but none of them was able to provide them a comfortable life. So they relied on funds from charitable associations. In his teenage years, he worked with John Grinder, the co-creator of neuro-linguistic programming. He promoted Grinder's neuro-linguistic programming by encouraging people to attend Grinder's seminars. Later, Grinder taught him the fundamental concepts of NLP.

At 20, he was at home most of the time, watching T.V. shows. Consequently, he gained an enormous amount of weight. His friend's insistence on losing weight changed his life. He transformed himself through the knowledge he had gained while working with Grinder.

Today, Robbins conducts self-improvement seminars on leading a healthy lifestyle, leadership skills and the gaining and management of wealth. He is a respectable coach and motivational speaker. He has written many books like 'The Unlimited Power,' 'Awakening the Giant Within' and 'Notes from a Friend.' He has a huge fan base.

Robbins has spoken in the House of Commons and has worked with Mother Teresa, Princess Diana, Michael Douglas, Andre Agassi, etc. He said that you must realize that your old bad habits are detrimental. He also advises how to get out of abusive relationships, how to eliminate alcohol and drug abuse or to deal with your fears and phobias.

Anthony Robbins made believe people in themselves and trust that they can do anything if they use their willpower. Sometimes, change is necessary to trigger haste to make the changes that will make things better. He inspired people to make changes to walk out of abusive relationships, to enhance their careers, to become wealthy, to lose weight, and to become healthy. His immense knowledge, experience and mastery only enhanced his success and fame.

CREATIVITY NEEDS A BIG DREAM

Chapter 5

Creativity needs a big dream

CREATIVITY NEEDS A BIG DREAM

Creativity and dreams are inseparable from each other. Without dreams, creativity cannot be harnessed and without creativity, dreams cannot be fulfilled. Creativity can be some type of discovery or innovation. It can be in the form of new research, a new book, a new painting or a new film, a new product, a new service, etc. If we dream something big, it means our unconscious mind wants to say something different, which we should not ignore. Dreams tell us the desires of our unconscious mind. Creativity helps us to shape our thoughts into reality. Both creativity and dreams need each other and move in the same direction.

Modern psychologist admit this and clarify that during dreams, our unconscious (intuitive) thoughts and memory take over. Dreams have been the creative source of many artists, writers, musicians and scientists in the history of creativity. Edgar Allen Poe's imaginative stories and poems were inspired by his nightmares. The German chemist, Friedrich August Kekune's discovery of the benzene molecule came from a dream in which he saw a snake of atoms that grabbed hold of its own tail, formed a circle. This led to the discovery of the benzene molecule that had a circular structure. To follow our creative path, we should follow our dreams.

The story of Sylvester Stallone is a story of his firm self-belief in his big dream. He followed his dream despite all the odds against him. Michael Sylvester Garden Zio Stallone was born in New York. His nerve was damaged during his difficult childbirth in which forceps had to be used to assist in Sylvester's delivery. This led to him having slurred speech. Sylvester and his younger brother, Frank, were raised in a hostile environment. He was emotionally deprived of parents and did not do well in school.

His mother told him that he didn't have a body he could work with. His father told him that he didn't have a brain. He was expelled from school thrice. His parents fought a lot and later divorced. He was sent to several foster homes. At last, he got admission in a special school for troubled children.

He wanted to inspire people who were going through the same troubles as he was. His big dream was to become an actor. He went to Miami State University to study drama, but his desire was so overwhelming that he decided to leave school. He headed straight to New York. He auditioned many times but his agent denied him a role, telling him that the business had no place for someone with an injured face. But he was determined to be an actor. He frequently fought with his wife during this difficult period.

He was craving for his big dream. He played small roles in a number of films and got a starring role in a pornographic production. He thought it might lead him to a bigger role. It was difficult for him to get a big role. Stallone discovered his skill for storytelling, he would spend time in the city library or stay home, writing stories, mainly inspiring stories. He got the idea of a character, Rocky Balboa, when watching a boxing match of the great Mohammad Ali, which inspired his scriptwriting. He wanted to play the character of Rocky Balboa, the starring role, himself. He often used to visualize the character as if he was playing it.

Stallone went to a casting being conducted by Robert Chartoff and Irwin Winkler. But he did not get the role, so he offered his manuscript. The team was quite impressed by his story. They offered Stallone a large amount of money to buy the material. However, Stallone agreed only on the condition that he play the starring role. Everyone agreed with him.

During shooting, the movie took a toll on his body, but he was steadfast in his faith.

The movie was a low-budget one. Stallone got his family and close friends to play small roles in the movies and production. When the movie was released, it was a big hit. It opened the doors for Sylvester Stallone's career in acting, writing and directing. He did over 40 films and is active even today, at 67. He was stubborn about what he wanted and he achieved his dream. He never gave up hope about achieving his dream. His imagination and constant effort made him achieve his big dream to be an actor. He chased his dream and his perseverance took him to his destiny.

Chapter 6

Creativity connects imagination and courage

Without imagination, we cannot exploit our creative potential. Creativity encourages us to take risks to share our ideas with the world. We are aware of the unlimited power within us and we want to exploit our potential to create what we want.

In this process, we follow up on our instincts and connect to our inner voice. We dare to take risks and want to share our knowledge with the world. We try to gain deep knowledge and hone our skills. When all the branches of the river connect to the main river, it finally merges into the sea at the end. Similarly, imaginative ideas connect to main ideas and bring a whole lot of useful ideas, and these useful and original ideas finally take the form of creativity.

Creativity discards waste ideas and selects only useful ideas. When we do what we love to do, we feel happy and are encouraged in our adventurous projects. We feel encouraged to take risks to implement our big ideas. There are times when we can face financial setbacks for our project funding and sometimes, we come up against social hurdles to meet our goals because our family and friends don't support us as they find our ideas odd or unreliable. Sometimes, we feel depressed and anxious due to unconscious blockages likes fear, anger, self-doubt, insecurity, low self-esteem, etc.

If we continue our journey with a positive attitude, these failures prove to be temporary phases in our life. When we sow some seeds and give it nourishment with sunrays, water and fertilizers, the seeds will take some time to grow into plants. Similarly, every goal takes some time to get the desired results. Thus, we should constantly work and take enough time to achieve our goal.

If the goal is big, then it will need a high degree of imaginative skills and courage and will take longer to get results but a small goal that doesn't need a very high degree of imagination will take less time. There are many examples like Amazon.com, Shakespeare's 'Othello,' Edison's invention of the electric bulb and Newton's theory of gravity, etc. These examples prove how creative projects connect imagination and courage and turn our dreams into realities.

Walt Disney's Disneyland is a good example of lofty imagination and courage. His story is like a real-world fairy tale. Disneyland, the amusement park for children, was the result of Walt Disney's vision. Walt Disney specialized in animation. He created the first ever animated movies like 'Mickey Mouse' and 'Snow White and the Seven Dwarfs.'

He is recognized for his big dream and his courage to turn that dream into reality.

Walt Disney was born in Chicago. He grew up with five siblings in a farm in Marceline, Missouri. From an early age, he was interested in art and drawing. At the age of 16, he joined Red Cross but was later fired. He moved to Kansas and worked for a creative advertising company but was fired from there too. So he created a film studio, Laugh-o-gram, but the studio closed due to financial instability.

Afterward, he opened a studio with his brother, Roy, and named it Disney Brother's Studio. Later, it was renamed Walt Disney Studio. He created 'Oswald, The Lucky Rabbit,' an animated movie, which became a hit. It proved to be one of the highest grossing movie of all times.

Walt had many business partnerships but was betrayed in most of his partnerships. Sometimes he became frustrated but still continued with his business. At a point in time when his business relationship with his brother was not cordial, he was on a train ride from Manhattan to Hollywood. That was when the idea of Mickey Mouse popped into his mind. He started working on the Mickey Mouse talking series of animated shorts. It was a big hit. And he created many others, like 'Silly Symphonies' which features music and some dialogue, stories like 'Three Little Pigs', 'Snow White and the Seven Dwarfs' (a full-length animated film), 'Bambi' etc.

In 1932, Disney was the first to bring cutting-edge, three-strip technicolour to the big screen. In 1933, his studio produced the 'Three Little Pigs', with its iconic song, 'Who 's afraid of the big bad wolf?'. It was a runaway success, eventually becoming the most successful animated short film of all time. His studio had become the king of the animated feature film. However, he was not satisfied with his success. He wanted to break new grounds with an animator feature. He turned to television.

He had big hits like 'Davy Crockett' and 'The Mickey Mouse Club.'

In 1934, he announced to the newspapers that his studio would be the first to put an animated feature film on the screen. His film required more than 160,000 paintings and the animators produced more than two million images in the course of the project. The estimated cost was $150,000 to $250,000. But he determined to make an animated film, whatever the cost. He made 'Snow White and The Seven Dwarfs' (a full-length animated film). Disney was not satisfied with his achievements and wanted to achieve more adventurous things as his imagination was running high and he had the courage to follow his dreams.

After the Second World War, Disney made 'Cinderella,' 'Alice in Wonderland' and 'Peter Pan' - all animation movies. Disney wanted to build a Disneyland park for children. Now Disneyland had become the magical land of his fantasy and big dreams. Two thousand five hundred men worked on the project and its estimated cost was around $17 million. Disneyland has become one of the most tourist popular destinations in the world.

Walt Disney's animation movies have been nominated for 13 Academy Awards, 29 Oscars, four Emmys, the Irving Halberd award, the Presidential Medal of Freedom and the French Legion of Honour.

In the words of Walt Disney, "All our dreams can come true, if we have the courage to pursue them."

Chapter 7

Creativity as a skill and the need for practice to polish it

Life is full of challenges. To overcome these challenges, we need to develop knowledge and specific skills. To enhance our skills, we need a supportive environment, and we need to enrol in courses and training as well. A prominent education psychologist, who studied mastery, wrote in 1985 that none of his subjects achieved expertise without a supportive environment and a long intensive period of training. This education came first from encouraging instructors and later, from demanding master teachers.

But the most important point is to keep practicing intensively in a disciplined manner. Practice can make us masters of our skills. Practice sparks our imagination and creativity. Because, to attain perfection, we think beyond our limitations and seek new ideas that were not there before. The more we practice, the better we become at getting new ideas. Psychologist K. Anders Ericsson, of Florida State University, conducted studies of experts in piano, violin, chess, bridge or athletics. The investigations revealed that a person's level of achievement correlated strongly with the amount of practice put in.

Creativity can be applied to any profession, whether it is sports, journalism, teaching, architecture, science, art, music, writing, cooking, singing, business, management, technology, etc. We need knowledge and skill to produce creative thought. However, if we don't put in practice with this knowledge and skills, we can't produce new ideas. If we put oil in the machines for them to run perfectly, then we can use that machine properly; likewise, if we don't put practice with the knowledge and skills that we have, we can't produce new ideas. The contribution of creative thought or skill can directly translate into career development and financial reward.

Creativity as a skill and the need for practice to polish it

Michael Jordan is recognized as a basketball icon in the field of sports. His knowledge and skills are superb. This amount of knowledge, skill and precision came only from constant practice, diligence and love for the game. He was born in Brooklyn, New York. He was the fourth of five children. As a child, he had a very close relationship with his father as they both bonded over the game of baseball. His older brother, Larry, used to play basketball. He followed in his brother's footsteps and chose basketball. They moved to North Carolina. Michael liked winning at the game.

Initially, he did not have adequate skills. So he was rejected from being part of the basketball team. He was determined to be part of the team and practice was his plan. He went to school early every day and arrived before everybody else did. He spent the morning practicing, shooting the hoop in the gym. He was so involved in practice that his physical education teacher had to drag him out of the gym when the first-period bell rang.

Michael again tried his luck in the team and was selected as a team member but was not allowed to play in interschool games. He tried even more to perfect himself. At last, he was selected for the junior basketball team and accepted the basketball scholarship offered by the University of North Carolina. He established himself as a skilled basketball player. He persisted to achieve what he wanted. He had a never-give-up attitude and for him, nothing was impossible. To utilize his potential, he practiced a lot and he played well under pressure. In the basketball court, according to Larry Bird, another basketball great, "He was God disguised as Michael Jordan."

He was the third pick in the National Basketball Association during the 1984 season. He bagged the Rookie of the Year title and started pulling the Chicago Bull's weight into the play off and captured many championship trophies. He was a constant pick in the NBA all-star games and brought pride to the United States in the Olympics. He was recognized as the best defensive player in the 1988 season, and was honoured with 'the most valuable player' award numerous times. He never gave up and practiced constantly, to polish his skills. His perfection in the game made him a basketball superstar.

Chapter-8

Creativity promotes innovation

Creativity connects new ideas and formulates useful and original concepts that are based on previous ideas. When we implement these ideas in a product or service and in a process, then we give it the name of Innovation. There are many examples in the history of innovation like the Wright brothers' aeroplane, Edison's electric bulb, Bill Gate's Microsoft, Steve Job's Apple Inc., Jeff Bezos' amazon.com, etc. Bezos and his wife (now ex-wife), MacKenzie Bezos left their lucrative jobs in New York's financial sector and set up the social networking site, amazon.com. Initially, they faced many obstacles but in just a few years, amazon.com was worth billions.

We know that creativity connects imaginative ideas. These ideas take the shape of innovation. Without creativity, innovation is not possible. Without creativity, imagination cannot be used. They are interwoven and follow each other; they are inseparable. Creativity is like a pot full of water; when we drink it, then it is innovation. High creativity leads to big innovation.

Some people use their creativity to solve social problems and they succeed in their objective. There are no conditions for creativity; it only needs one goal at a time. Some people use their creativity with many goals at a time. They work at their current job and innovate in their spare time to solve social problems. Imran Khan is a good example of how creativity and innovation solve social problems. Today, Imran Khan is a well-known name in India. He is a 34-year-old mathematics teacher from Alwar (Rajasthan). He created 52 free educational mobile apps and donated them to the nation for educational purposes.

Prime Minister Mr. Narendra Modi thanked him for his venture from Wimbledon in London. Khan had no formal training in computers. He gained all the knowledge himself through Google and his engineer brother's books. When Khan was free after school, he learned about HTML and designed websites.

In 2005, he designed his first website - www.gktalks.com. After that he created more than 100 websites, but maintained only two of them- gktalks and gyan manjari. Creating websites was not his job but he took it up as a hobby for a social cause. In the words of Imran Khan, "I like to make cool and creative interfaces. I like challenges. Without challenges, I can't work. Web development is my hobby."

Imran's story is an inspiration for all those who want to pursue their passion but are unable to follow their instincts owing to circumstances. If they are determined, they can find success in doing something that is inspired by their creativity. All of us are creative but our creative passion doesn't flourish because we are not able to recognize it early. Thus, we can't exploit our potential. Sometimes, this hidden creative spirit comes out as a hobby and takes the shape of innovation, which is what happened in the case of Imran Khan.

Most of our hobbies are hidden creative energies which should not be ignored. Some people convert their hobby into a profession and others want to pursue their hobby as a profession. They can develop their hobby for a social cause, like Imran Khan who developed his hobby of creating websites and apps for social causes and gained fame. He developed his creative flair into an innovation.

Chapter 9

Types of creativity - scientific or artistic

Creativity is a broad concept. It does not require general skills but is based on specific skills and knowledge. These skills can be related to arts or sciences or any other area of life like business, sports, music, fashion, design, film making, etc. Creativity depends on many factors like the level of hunger we have for knowledge and skills, the level of challenges, our emotional and intellectual development, the environment in which we live and how we think and act.

Psychologist Simonton gave us the concept of little creativity (little c) and big creativity (big c). Little c includes daily problem solving and the ability to adapt to change. For example – amazon. com, yahoo.com, PayTM, etc. They bring change which provides comfort to people. This type of creativity does not need a high degree of knowledge and skills or great effort like big creativity. When we dream big and our hunger level for knowledge and skills are high, then we are highly creative souls. For example, Albert Einstein 'theory of relativity, the Wright brothers' aircraft and Watson & Crick's 'double helix model.' Big creativity has the capacity to bring revolution into the lives of people. This type of creativity needs a high degree of knowledge and a lot of effort and time management. This type of creativity brings radical and unexpected changes which surprises people. Big creativity has the level of something like the Nobel prize and Pulitzer prize.

Creativity can be scientific or artistic. Scientific creativity needs a high challenge and a lot of effort and time. It requires a high degree of knowledge and cognitive engagement with abstract and semantic information, primarily through reasoning. For example, Thomas

Edison's invention of the electric bulb, Graham Bell's telephone, Damadian's discovery of the MRI, mathematician John Nash's discovery of method of game theory etc. But artistic creativity needs emotional expression in the form of imagination, beauty and fantasy. These emotional expressions take the shape of some kind of writing, painting and any other imaginative works of art. For example, Shakespeare's 'Othello', the '9th symphony' of Wolfgang Amadeus Mozart, Leonardo da Vinci's 'Mona Lisa' painting etc. It does not require specific intellectual knowledge. It needs specific skills that can be polished through disciplined practice.

Within psychological research, the most common type of creativity is that of scientific versus artistic creativity, particularly in personality-based studies on creativity (Barron & Harrington, 1981; Feist, 1998). Highly creative people show greater openness to novel experiences, are attracted to complexity, and display heightened aesthetic sensibilities. Some recent research has revealed though that 'openness to experience' is predictive of creative achievement in the arts whereas 'intellect' is predictive of the same in the sciences (Kaufman et al., 2016). Highly creative people experience greater openness to experience.

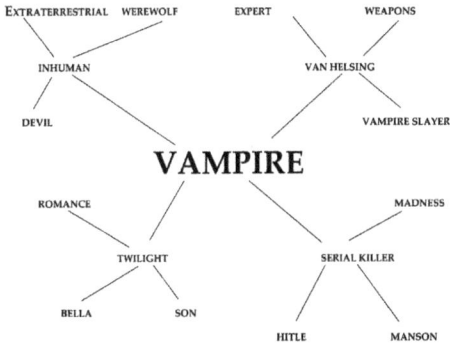

```
EXTRATERRESTRIAL   WEREWOLF        EXPERT              WEAPONS

         INHUMAN                   VAN HELSING

    DEVIL                              VAMPIRE SLAYER

              VAMPIRE

       ROMANCE                           MADNESS

           TWILIGHT              SERIAL KILLER

     BELLA          SON
                              HITLE        MANSON
```

Chapter 10

Different ways to develop creativity

The development of our creativity leads to a change in our thinking pattern, beliefs and attitude. It brings awareness and clarity about our purpose in life. It strengthens our focus and self-control. We learn gratitude and let go of attitude. We don't worry about what is happening around us. We are happy and at peace, and focused on finding our destiny. Our motivation and determination become so strong that we are encouraged to take on challenges; our empathy is very strong too.

Creativity is our hidden treasure which needs to be acknowledged by us. If this hidden treasure can be developed in a disciplined manner, we can utilize our full potential. Generally, people use their left hemisphere, which is the logical and ruling brain. We do not use our right hemisphere for our routine work. If we use both hemispheres well, we can utilize the potential of our entire brain. To develop creativity, idea generation is the first stage of the creative process. We use both our right and left hemispheres. The left hemisphere is rational, slow, ruling, sequential and cognitive while the right hemisphere is imaginative, fast, random and spontaneous.

In 2009, neuroscientist Sharon Thompson-Schill of the University of Pennsylvania and her colleagues proposed that creative inspiration might benefit from a state of lower cognitive control, i.e. fewer restrictions on our thoughts and behaviour. When we abandon our ruling centre prefrontal cortex, which is involved in conscious monitoring, self-inhibition and the evaluation of the rightness and wrongness of actions you are about to implement, quieten down; this state is called hypofrontality. Another part of the brain, the medial prefrontal cortex, which is part of a default mode network, gets turned on. This state boosts creative idea generation.

Creativity can be learned, developed and applied. It is a process of generating and implementing new ideas. It is a skill that requires practice to develop in a disciplined manner. These skills can be enhanced with specific tools and techniques. There is a need for creativity in innovative technology for the growth of the economy.

Many prestigious business schools such as Harvard and Stanford have added courses to their curricula to develop creative potential. Many corporations such as Coca Cola, Reliance and Citi group have chief innovation officers on their leadership team. Fortune 500 companies, including PepsiCo, Bristol-Meyers & Quibb, Aetna and Marriott, now put employee through creativity training programs and videos. It is a skill that is needed for the survival of a business in a competitive environment. Employees are trained to use various tools and techniques to think outside the box.

Different ways to develop creativity

1. Creativity requires focus, a relaxed mind and imagination. Lorenza Colza, a Dutch psychologist, investigated meditation on creative thinking. According to him, open monitoring or non-directive mindfulness, which focuses on observing thoughts that arise in mind in a non-judgmental way and accepting the circumstances of the present moment, leads to free-flowing ideas and boosts the imagination network. So mindfulness develops our inner world as well as our outer world. It is one of the greatest tools to access our creative emotions like gratitude, empathy, forgiveness, self-acceptance, etc. as well as our focus and self-control towards the external environment. It helps us to boost our creativity to produce new and original ideas.

2. Brainstorming is another way to produce random and non-linear ideas. According to the Oxford Dictionary, brainstorming is 'a spontaneous group discussion to produce ideas and ways of solving problems.' In brainstorming sessions, a group of six to ten people focus on a problem and discuss the problem. The leader of the group invites ideas from every person in the group. They write down all the ideas and then select useful ideas and combine them.

The term was coined in 1941 by the BBDO advertising agency's executive vice president, Alex F. Osborn (1888-1966), who defined it as 'a creative conference (group discussion) for producing a list of ideas which can be subsequently evaluated and further processed'. Osborn explained the ground rules for brainstorming, in his book (1953) 'Applied Imagination': 1) focus on quality 2) withhold criticism 3) welcome wild and unusual ideas 4) combine and improve ideas. Osborn found that when these rules were followed, unexpected creative ideas were produced, which in turn gave rise to a greater number of useful ideas.

3. Creative writing is a great source for generating new ideas. Before writing, we should know about the subject on which we expect new and original ideas. This knowledge can be gathered through books, audiotapes, the internet, etc. We should write after waking up early, when our subconscious mind is active. Write from your heart without judgement and trust your intuition.

   The French author Gustav Flaubert (1821-1880) once told his young pupil, Guy de Maupassant (1850-1893) that knowing the subject is vital for all creative work. We need to collect sufficient information. We can write down important findings so that unusual ideas crop up. After writing down important findings, we should connect this information with our main idea.

Writing requires the application of the analytical, rational, left side of the brain. While your left hemisphere is occupied, your right hemisphere (the creative side) is given the freedom to wander and play. (Grothaus, 2015). The father of psychoanalysis, Sigmund Freud compared creative writing with daydreaming.

4. Training your brain for dreaming while asleep and daydreaming can enlist your subconscious mind to work on a problem that is bothering you. Albert Einstein pictured himself running along a light wave, which led to his theory of special relativity. Tim Burton daydreamed his way to Hollywood success.

Dreams have been the creative source for many artists, writers, musicians and scientists in the history of creativity. Edgar Allen Poe's imaginative stories and poems were inspired by his nightmares. To follow our creative path, we should train ourselves to dream.

In western psychology, here is how we harness our dreams:

a) Write down your problem as a brief phrase or sentence and place this note next to your bed. Also, keep a pen and paper and perhaps a flashlight.

b) Review the problem for a few minutes before going to bed.

c) Once in bed, visualize the problem as a concrete image if possible.

d) Tell yourself you want to dream about the problem as you drift off to sleep.

e) Arrange objects connected to the problem on your night table or on the wall across from your bed.

f) On awakening, lie quietly before getting out of bed. Note whether you recall any part of the dream. Write it down.

g) At bedtime, picture yourself dreaming about the problem, awakening and writing on your bedside notepad. (Originally published in: Scientific American Mind 23 (1), 58-64 (winter 2014)).

5. We can generate ideas through mind mapping. British psychologist Tony Buzan (Middlesex, 1942) expanded the technique in his books 'Use Your Head' and 'The Mind Map Book.'

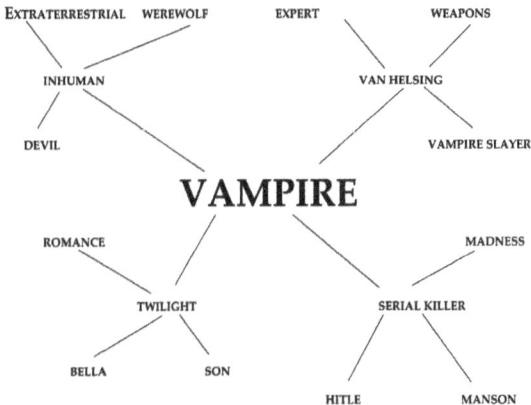

EXTRATERRESTRIAL   WEREWOLF   EXPERT   WEAPONS

    INHUMAN   VAN HELSING

DEVIL   VAMPIRE SLAYER

VAMPIRE

ROMANCE   MADNESS

    TWILIGHT   SERIAL KILLER

BELLA   SON

HITLE   MANSON

In a nutshell, the basic set of rules or guidelines recommended by Buzan include the following:

Take a sheet of blank paper and write your main word or keyword in the centre, leaving as much empty space around it as you can. For instance, write down the word VAMPIRE. Think of several words related to your central or basic word. For example – blood, monster, inhuman, vampirette, Van Helsing and undead. Write down these words around the central word (vampire). Connect each associated word to the main or central word using a line. Repeat the process and, in each new level, associate each associated word with new words or concepts to come up with a whole different level of related words, each one connected with lines that ultimately lead to the central or basic word.

Bill Gates and Steve Jobs would get creative success through mind mapping. They generated new ideas through teamwork in which every member contributed to a new project or job.

6. You should take some rest if you are not able to solve your problem on any project after working hard on it. We can lose our focus and concentration if we don't stop work. When you are searching for a new solution to a problem or some kind of new ideas, just take a break, put your problem out of your mind completely and indulge in an activity which gives you immense pleasure like playing an instrument, taking a shower, listening to classical music, going for a walk or sailing. It relaxes your brain and distracts you. It stimulates your unconscious mind and you can find creative ideas for your project or problem. Einstein used to play the violin to find creative ideas while taking a break from a project.

7. If you want to raise your creativity level, you need to concentrate on divergent thinking. It enhances

random and non-linear thinking. Convergent thinking is its opposite. It promotes logical thinking. Convergent thinking considers the cause and effect of any concept. It is about thinking in a sequential manner. Divergent thinking promotes spontaneous ideas. Its concept is: 'What if.......?' It gives you the freedom for imagination and non-linear and spontaneous thinking.

Divergent thinking links you to Walt Disney's world. It promotes the fluency of many ideas, the flexibility of ideas and elaboration in which we can expand ideas separately and produce originality, which means fresh and unique ideas.

8. Usually, highly creative people follow their passion. If we follow our passion, it stimulates our unconscious drive to do something different. These unconscious drives produce intense inspiration and efforts which help us to achieve our passion or dream. Latest science supports the importance of

passion in achieving any personally meaningful goal.

'The Colour Purple' author, Alice Walker, acknowledged that she fell in love with her imagination. "And if you fall in love with the imagination, you understand that it is a free spirit," she said. "It will go anywhere."

Thomas Edison said that genius is '1 percent inspiration and 99 percent perspiration'. Passion, inspiration and effort push each other in the same direction. They spark creative ideas. Thomas Yorker's passion for music started after he heard music of The Beatles; he then began to play guitar.

9. We can enhance creativity through exercise. It secretes our feel-good hormones, endorphins. When we feel great, we think creatively. Exercise uses our brain muscles. The more we use the muscles, the more creative we are. Exercise releases our anxiety,

boosts self-esteem, calms the mind and encourages us to do something different.

Creativity is stunted by stress. By reading, drawing, keeping our mind engaged in stimulating conversation and participating in group debates on exciting topics, we can create new ideas. Physical activities like yoga, walking, running, swimming, cycling, dancing, playing tennis, squash or golf increase blood flow to the brain and supply more oxygen, thereby boosting creativity. If a creative person exercises intensely, a story, a painting or some new big idea will come to him. He will find great ideas for his creative projects and feel great joy.

Haruki Murakami is one of Japan's most celebrated novelists and the author of books like 'Kafka on the Shore' and 'What I talk about when I talk about running.' He is also a serious athlete who runs at least one marathon a year. When Murakami is writing a novel, he says he runs or swims for at least an hour a day.

10. Travel is a unique way to enhance creativity. When you explore other areas of the world, you face new opportunities to interact with other people of different cultures. It nurtures your mind and brings new ideas. You want to exploit new areas of your life which have not been used before. It inspires your creativity.

Chapter 11

Conclusion

In conclusion, creativity is about promoting ideas that are new and original, that are based on previous ideas. Creativity is a universal phenomenon that everyone has an opportunity to exploit. It can change our destiny. We connect with our inner voice. Some people follow their inner voice and get what they want but, in some people, it remains a hidden talent that is not going to be used, and they are deprived of happiness and prosperity of life. They live their lives ignorant about their capabilities and strengths.

Creativity has many aspects. We cannot define creativity in a single word. It is a broader concept which overlaps many things. Self-awareness is required to realize our strengths and weaknesses. When we are self-aware about our unlimited potential, we strive to use our creative potential. We get inspiration from our surroundings in which we have family, friends, work colleagues, school, etc. Oprah Winfrey realized her creative potential when she went to live with her father. She learned her communication skills from her grandmother. She kept progressing in life and became a famous talk show personality and celebrity.

We cannot change our past but we should learn from our mistakes and ensure that we do not repeat them in the future. Anthony Robbins did that. He suffered from binge eating. His self-transformation made him a life coach. Robbins not only learnt from his mistakes but also guided people on how to live a healthy lifestyle. When we determine to do something challenging, creativity sparks our new ideas, which help us to make changes to meet our challenges.

Creativity is a skill and with constant practice, we can generate out-of-the-box thinking. When we continuously practice, our unconscious mind takes over and we get creative solutions or ideas for our problems. Michael Jordan's determination and persistence made him a king in basketball. Despite many rejections, he did not give up. His stubbornness propelled him to become a superstar in sports.

Creativity chases big dreams. Without challenges, creativity cannot be stimulated. To execute our big project, there may be many difficulties which can arise, like lack of funds to execute the project, lack of environmental support, lack of time, etc. If we have patience, courage and persistence to complete our projects, like Walt Disney did, there is no possibility of failing. Walt Disney's lofty imagination and unbounded courage to implement his big plan made him a unique and immortal name in the history of animated movies.

Sometimes, creativity turns our adversities into opportunities. Sometimes adversities like illness, death, accidents, financial instability, divorce, etc. suddenly arise. There are times when we are shocked at these unexpected adversities and cannot absorb the shock.

How to be creative and change your life

We become traumatized by unfortunate incidents and there is a void within us. Creative therapies like writing, painting, sculpture and music help us to fill these voids and help us to focus on our goal. We start a new phase in life filled with happiness and success. This is what happened to J.K. Rowling. Her dear mother's death, her divorce and poverty made her life difficult and miserable but her passion for creative writing turned her adversities into opportunities. Today she is a billionaire.

Creativity is not the virtue of just artists or writers; we all are creative. Creativity can be scientific or artistic, like Einstein, Bill Gates, Shakespeare or Mozart. Creativity can be small or big. Generally, big creativity requires very high imagination, effort and time. Big creativity can change the world and little creativity helps us to solve our daily problems. Creativity develops motivation and leadership skills. It opens up new opportunities to exploit and brings success.

Creativity can be enhanced in different ways. In mind mapping, we concentrate on a given problem and write down different words related to central words. Through mind mapping, we can get free-flowing ideas. However, in brainstorming, we think in non-random and non-linear ways to produce new ideas. We write down even wild and unexpected ideas. In the end, we select appropriate and useful ideas from the list of ideas and can get creative solutions for our projects or challenges.

Dreaming and the creative process are connected. While dreaming, our unconscious mind takes over the conscious mind, which is a precondition for idea generation. Our conscious mind is less active when we sleep and the unconscious mind is active then. We should visualize our problem before going to bed. While sleeping, our unconscious mind searches for solutions for the visualized problem. After waking up, we should write down whatever ideas pop up in our dream.

When we work on a project or process and are unable to find a solution to the problem, we should take a break and indulge in some pleasurable activity. Our unconscious mind takes over and we find creative solutions. Steve Jobs used to walk when taking a break from work. Travel is also an excellent way to stimulate our unconscious mind. It enhances our creative ideas. We travel to unknown or new zones and spark our creative flame.

Creativity is a good master when we use it properly. It exploits our brain power. It promotes the activation of a new neural network in our brains. It sparks creative ideas. We can bring changes in our lives and encourage others to changes their lives as well. We can even change the world via these big ideas through innovations or discoveries.

References

Bono, de edward, "the mechanism of mind: understand how your mind works to maximise memory and creative potential", vermilion, an imprint of ebury publishing, london.

Parr, a. J. (2013), "How to develop super creativity: boost your creative super powers in five easy steps!", Published by grapevine books/ediciones de la parra.

Stuart, sullins, m. A. (2012), "Experience the now: how to increase your level of consciousness," isbn: 978-0-98467674-3

Lochuteman davids (2016)," edison 's way: the inventor's rules to unlock, unfold and expand your creativity," copyspring

Hunt, michelle (2015), "creativity: innovation: simple, proven tips & tricks to improve your creative writing."

Scientific american (2015), "inspired! The science of creativity", scientific american publication, isbn:978-1-4668-5896-1.

Kaufman, barry, scott & gregoire, carolyn (2016), "wired to create: discover the 10 things, great artists, writers and innovators do differently", vermilion, london.

Dispenza, dr. Joe (2014), "you are the placebo: making your mind matter," hay house inc, usa.

Johnson, kevin, (2016), "motivational stories of determination, perseverance and success."

Kennedy, alexander (2017), "disney: making magic," fritzen publishing llc.

Jefferson kristi (2015), "brain training: 55 techniques to exercise your brain, increase your brain power and improve your memory", isbn-10:1507823401.

Collins.Brayn (2018), "the power of creativity: learning how to build lasting habits, face your fears and change your life (book1)", edited by command +z content and beth grosby.

Abraham, anna (2018), "the neuroscience of creativity (cambridge fundamental of neuroscience in psychology)," cambridge university press, leeds beckett university, u.K.

Mihaly csikszentmi halyi, "creativity: flow and the psychology of discovery and invention," harper collins e-books.

Buzan, tony, (2004), "mind maps at work: how to be the best at work and still have time to play," thorsons, an imprint of harper collins publishers limited, london.

Seppala, emma, (2016), "how to apply the science of happiness to accelerate your success," piatkus, london, isbn:978-0-349-40547-6.

How to be creative and change your life

Bono, de. Edward, "how to have creative ideas: 62 exercises to develop the mind", vermillion, london.

Afterwords

If you enjoyed this book, please rate it and leave a short review. A review like yours helps me write more books like this one.

Finally, if you have feedback about this book, you can always email info@ creativityincolour.Com. I would love to hear from you.